Thank you
Enjoy!
Jasmine Crowe

Everybody Eats

Written by Jasmine Crowe
Illustrated by Nadia Fisher

Everybody Eats

All rights reserved. No part of this publication may be reproduced, stored in a retrieval system, or transmitted in any form or by any means, electronic, mechanical, photocopying, recording, or otherwise, without written permission of the copyright owner, except for the use of brief quotations in a book review.

Text copyright © 2021 by Jasmine Crowe
Illustrations copyright © 2021 by Nadia Fisher
Book design by Leah Marché

Published by Life's A Journey Publishing
First printing, 2021

ISBN 978-0-578-94614-6

To request permissions or for other information, please contact:

Life's A Journey Publishing
c/o The Gathering Spot
384 Northyards Boulevard NW
Unit 100
Atlanta, Georgia 30313
United States
info@everybodyeatsbook.com

everybodyeatsbook.com

Carter knew two things about Saturdays: there wouldn't be school, but there would be work.

This Saturday, Carter, her mother and father were volunteering at the **food bank**. Although Carter had never been to the **food bank**, last year she had helped her parents find cans that they could donate around the holidays.

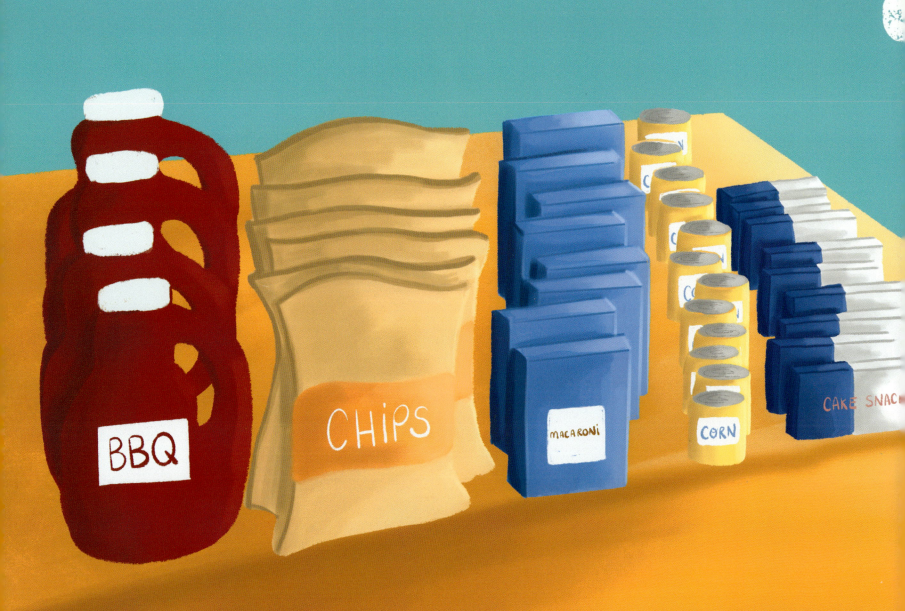

When they arrived at the **food bank**, a lady in charge told them that they would pack bags and hand them out.

"Every bag should have a gallon of barbeque sauce, a bag of kettle potato chips, a box of superhero-shaped macaroni noodles, a miniature can of corn, and a box of low fat Ding Dongs."

"What meal could be made out of these things?" Carter thought.

Nothing like the spaghetti and meatballs Carter's dad had made last night.

Carter and her parents filled up their bags. Once they were finished, Carter looked inside the bag and frowned.

"Would this fill an empty tummy?" she worried.

After all the bags were packed, they began handing them out. All types of people were there for food: tall; short; old and young; big families and small families. All different races were at the **food bank**.

Carter guessed that the only thing everyone had in common was that they were hungry.

Carter held out her last bag to a tall man, but when she looked next to him, she was surprised to see her friend from school.

"Emma?!" Carter exclaimed. Her friend stared back, just as surprised.

Emma's dad looked panicked, but Carter's mom suggested they go talk over by the door.

Emma looked down; she was embarrassed. "My Dad lost his job, and my mom has trouble supporting all four of us. Sometimes we need help."

"I understand, Emma. I promise not to tell anyone if you don't want me to," Carter said.

Emma gave her a big hug and told Carter thank you. Emma took her bag and waved goodbye to Carter from the door.

On the way back home, Carter sat in the back seat. She tried to come up with a solution for how to help Emma. "Maybe I could give Emma all my lunches, or her family could come live with us. We have plenty of food."

Carter's mom and dad shared a look. "Carter, you need to eat lunch, too," her dad said.

"So you can grow big and strong," her dad continued. "And Emma's family has their own home they want to live in," her mom added.

"Then what can I do?" Carter asked, feeling very small and so sad.

Carter's parents shared another look. "We'll look online once we get home. We want to help too, Carter."

When they arrived at home, all three of them crowded around the computer. They scrolled through pages of ideas until they found a book, *Everybody Eats*.

Carter's family read through the pages before ordering it.

"Can I do this?" she asked. "Will you help me?"

Her parents nodded.

Sunday Carter leapt out of bed and quickly ran through her morning routine.

Teeth brushed and hair braided...

... Carter slid down the banister to open the front door.

Outside, a brown package waited. Her book! Carter could hardly wait before she tore it open.

Carter turned through the pages before pulling a notebook out of her backpack.

She would have to be ready to tell people what they could do to stop hunger, and she knew the first place she would go...

"To the grocery store!" Carter cried, as her parents trailed behind her.

In the car on the way there, Carter turned through the pages of her book until they arrived.

Once inside, Carter made her way toward Manager Pete, who had been at the store as long as Carter's family had shopped there.

"Hi, Mr. Pete!" Carter said.

"Well, hey there, Carter," Pete replied. "What's on the agenda today? Cookie dough? Pie crust?" Carter shook her head.

"Not today. I actually have a question for you!"

Pete smiled. "Sure! I'll help any way I can."

"What happens to the food that nobody buys?" Carter asked.

"Well, we donate what we can, but sometimes we have to send it to the dump!" he responded.

"Even if the food hasn't gone bad?" Carter asked.

Pete paused. He looked a little surprised by her question. "Yes."

"What if, instead of throwing that delicious food away, you gave it to a charity for feeding the hungry?"

Pete's eyes got so wide they could have been dinner plates.

"Well, we'd love to Carter, but if we gave them the food, we might get sued."

"That's not true, Mr. Pete. See here." Carter opened her book. "It says right here that under **The Good Samaritan Act of 1996** that if you donate your food in **good faith**, you can't get sued."

Mr. Pete pulled down his glasses and read the pages over her shoulder. When he finished, he had a big smile. "I had no idea!"

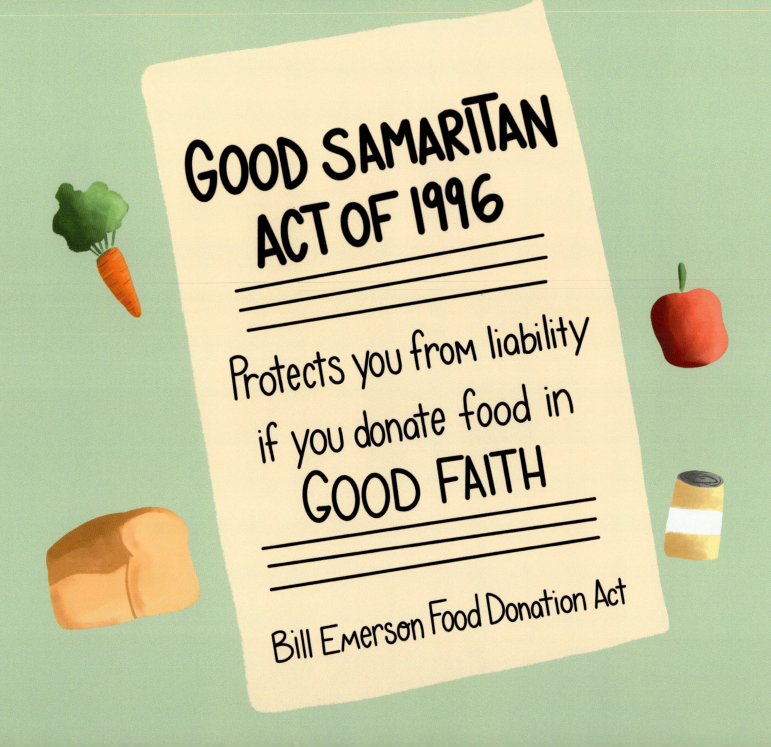

"Will you talk to your boss about helping with food waste, Mr. Pete?" Carter asked, doing her best puppy dog eyes.

"There's no need for that sad look. We'd love to help. I'll talk to the owner right away." And with that, Mr. Pete disappeared into the back room.

"I have to get ready to go to one more place," Carter said. "Back to school."

Carter had never been to Principal Noor's office, but on Monday morning, she arrived with a notebook filled with the facts she had learned from her book.

An hour before the first bell, she stood outside the office.

"You can do it, Carter. We know you can," her mom said.

Carter's mom and dad each took one of her hands. Together, they went inside the Principal's office.

PRINCIPAL

Principal Noor sat at her desk going through huge stacks of paper, but when she saw Carter, she sat up straight.

"Carter," she said in her deep voice. "I've heard that you wanted to meet with me."

"Yes, ma'am." Carter took a deep breath and pulled out her book.

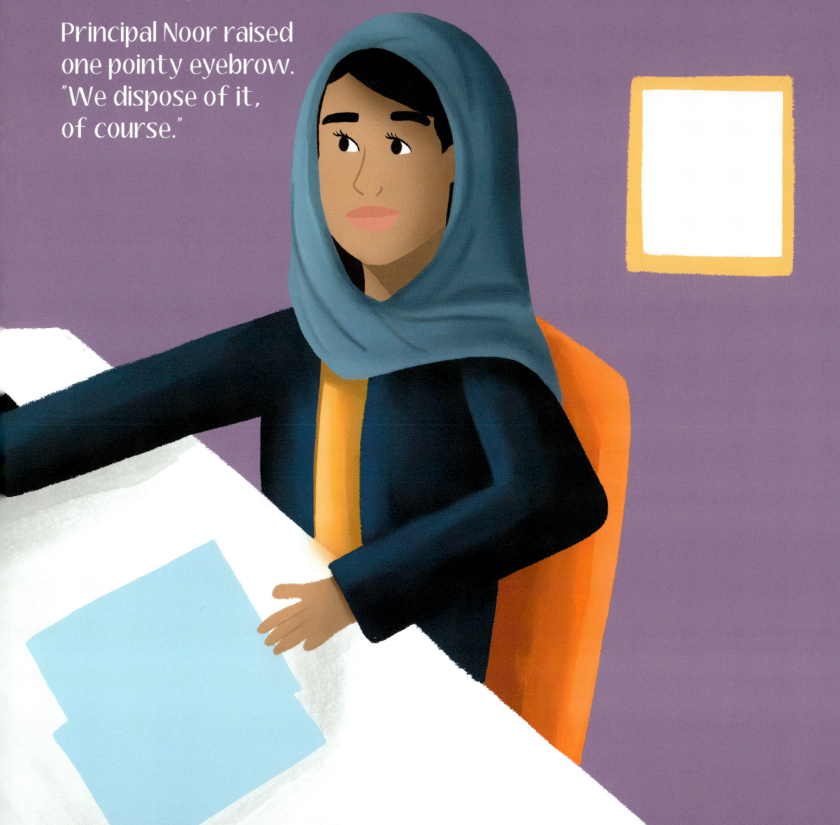

"I wanted to ask you what you do with the food that doesn't get cooked for lunch. Or what happens to the food that isn't eaten at those fancy buffets?"

Principal Noor raised one pointy eyebrow. "We dispose of it, of course."

"But in school, we recycle because we really care about the environment, right?"

For a second Principal Noor looked pleased. "That's exactly right. However, I fail to see how the two are related."

Carter placed her book out for Principal Noor to read.

"One way is that there are students at our school who are hungry, and they could use that food! Just because they show up to school doesn't mean that they have enough food at home."

Carter stopped herself before she mentioned Emma. It wasn't her place to tell what Emma's family was going through, even if she really wanted to.

Principal Noor looked at her curiously. Carter continued.

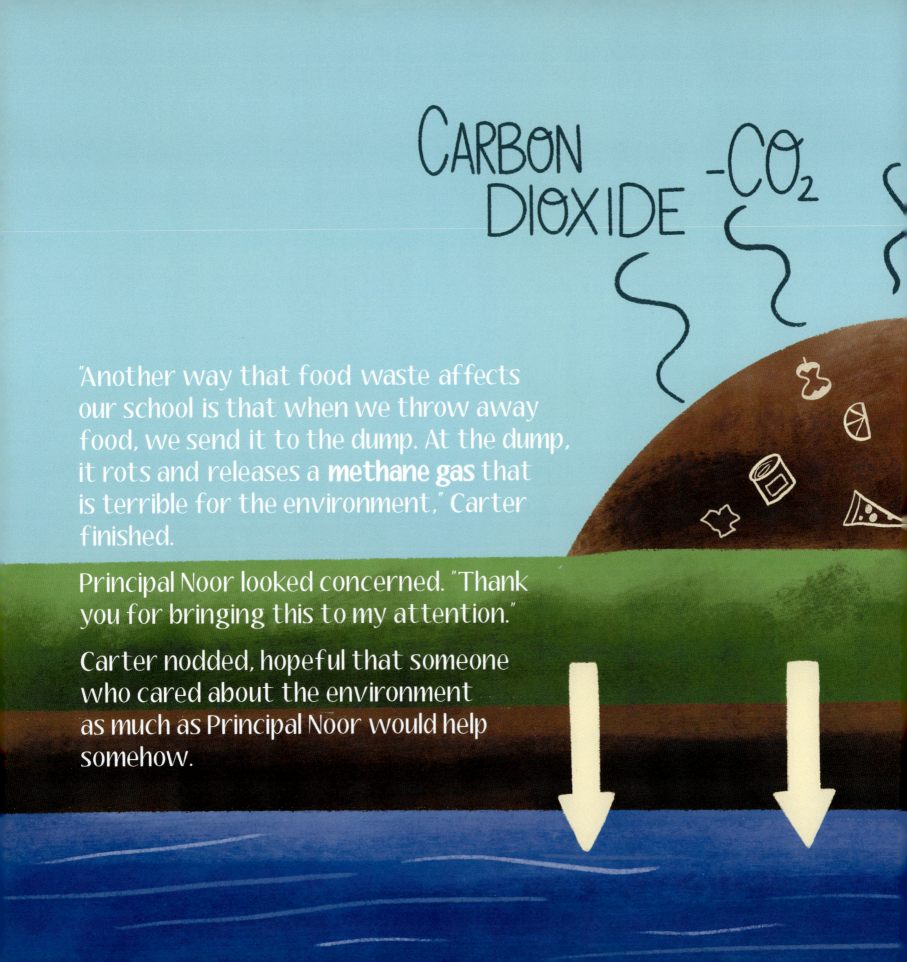

CARBON DIOXIDE -CO₂

"Another way that food waste affects our school is that when we throw away food, we send it to the dump. At the dump, it rots and releases a **methane gas** that is terrible for the environment," Carter finished.

Principal Noor looked concerned. "Thank you for bringing this to my attention."

Carter nodded, hopeful that someone who cared about the environment as much as Principal Noor would help somehow.

CH₄ - METHANE GAS

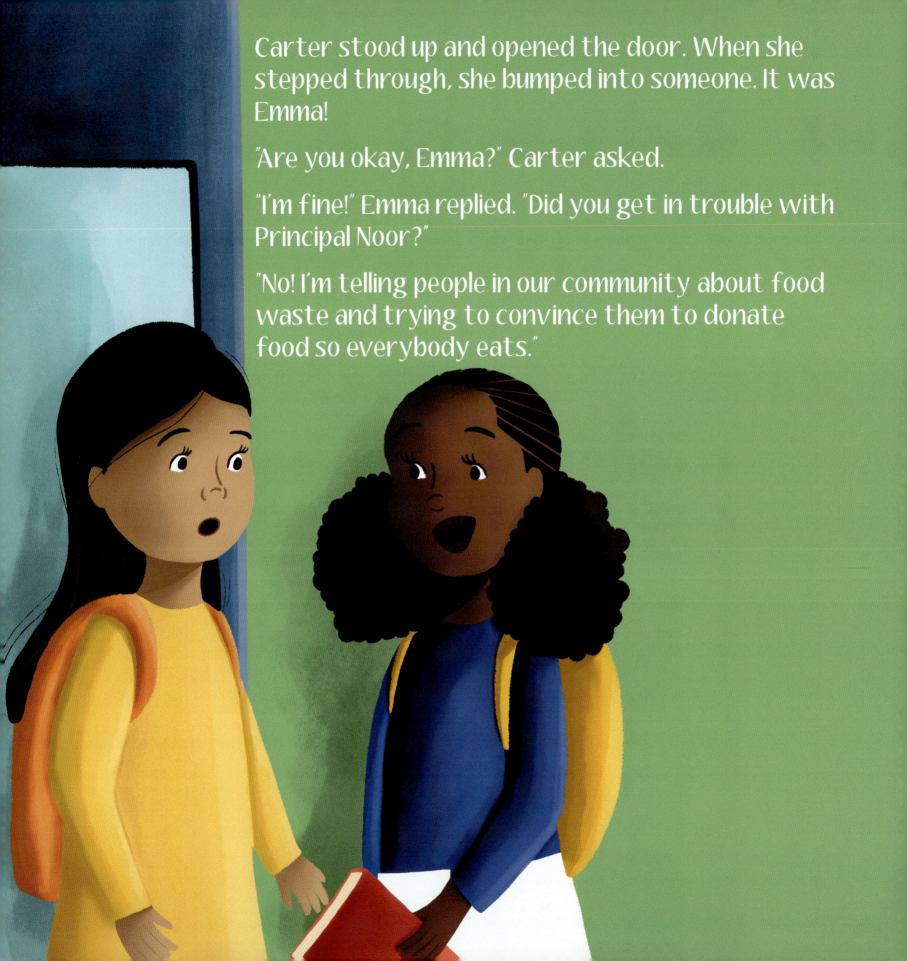

Carter stood up and opened the door. When she stepped through, she bumped into someone. It was Emma!

"Are you okay, Emma?" Carter asked.

"I'm fine!" Emma replied. "Did you get in trouble with Principal Noor?"

"No! I'm telling people in our community about food waste and trying to convince them to donate food so everybody eats."

"Is this because you saw us at the **food bank**?" Emma asked. She looked embarrassed again.

"Sort of," Carter said. "It's because no one should go to bed hungry. If I can help, I'm going to—"

Before Carter could finish, Emma gave her a big hug. "You're a real friend, Carter."

Carter hugged her back only to hear the dinging of the first bell. Emma waved goodbye, heading to class.

Carter felt herself be lifted up on her dad's shoulders while her mom clapped for her.

"We're so proud of you, Carter. You're not just a good friend to Emma; you're a good friend to all the hungry people in our community. I can only imagine what you will do in the future." Carter's mom said.

"I have an idea about what I'll do next," Carter said.
"But you'll have to wait until next Saturday to find out!"

The End

Dear Reader,

By purchasing this book, you've also taken the first step in stopping hunger, just like Carter.

Please know that a meal has been bought for someone hungry with the money you spent on this book.

Stay tuned for more of Carter's adventures and to find out how you can help fight against hunger.

Glossary

Food bank: A charity organization that gives free food to people in need.

The Good Samaritan Act 1996: The Bill Emerson Good Samaritan Good Donation Act was created to encourage and to protect people who donate food in good faith. It was signed by President Bill Clinton in 1996.

Good faith: To have no bad intentions.

Methane gas: When our food rots in landfills, it releases a type of gas called methane. Too much of this gas is really bad for the earth's atmosphere.

Food insecure: A person is food insecure when they do not know where their next meal is coming from.

Visit EverybodyEatsBook.com

Resources are available for kids and teachers, including coloring sheets, games and lesson guides.

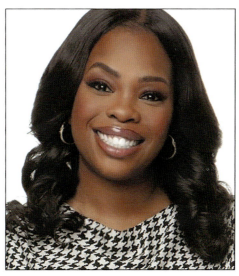

JASMINE CROWE

Acknowledgments

Thank you to Sydney Brown, Ashley Summerall, Leah Marché, my family, friends and my fiancé for all the times you listened and helped me through this process.